Do You See a Green Dinosaur?

Seed Learning

red

yellow

orange

green

blue

purple

black

white

Do you see
a green dinosaur?

Yes, I see
a green dinosaur.

Do you see
a yellow ball?

Yes, I see
a yellow ball.

Do you see
a blue fish?

Yes, I see
a blue fish.

Do you see
a red apple?

Yes, I see
a red apple.

Do you see
a purple car?

Yes, I see
a purple car.

Do you see a black and white panda?

Yes, I see a black and white panda.

Let's learn more about Laos.

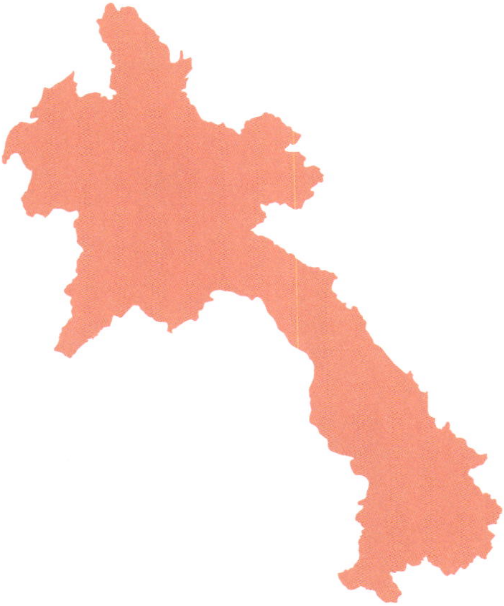

Tam mak hoong